SANDY SOYKE

Unlocking the Magic of Crystals for Beginners

Copyright © 2022 by Sandy Soyke

All rights reserved. No part of this publication may be reproduced, stored or transmitted in any form or by any means, electronic, mechanical, photocopying, recording, scanning, or otherwise without written permission from the publisher. It is illegal to copy this book, post it to a website, or distribute it by any other means without permission.

Sandy Soyke asserts the moral right to be identified as the author of this work.

Sandy Soyke has no responsibility for the persistence or accuracy of URLs for external or third-party Internet Websites referred to in this publication and does not guarantee that any content on such Websites is, or will remain, accurate or appropriate.

Designations used by companies to distinguish their products are often claimed as trademarks. All brand names and product names used in this book and on its cover are trade names, service marks, trademarks and registered trademarks of their respective owners. The publishers and the book are not associated with any product or vendor mentioned in this book. None of the companies referenced within the book have endorsed the book.

First edition

This book was professionally typeset on Reedsy.
Find out more at reedsy.com

"Crystals are like Potato Chips. You can't have just one"

—Earth Family Crystals —

Contents

Acknowledgement	ii
Unlocking The Magic of Crystals For Beginners	iii
Introduction: How my Journey into Crystals Began	iv
1 Crystals - A Little History, A Lot of Magic	1
2 Crystals and Their Specific Healing Powers	9
3 How to Recharge Your Crystals	26
4 Understanding What Crystals Are Right for You	30
5 Quick Easy Crystal Guide for Common Health Issues	37
Credits	40
Selected Bibliography	42
About the Author	43

Acknowledgement

I truly appreciate Kindness.
  I appreciate people checking up on me.
  I appreciate a quick message.
  I appreciate those who ask if I'm okay.
  I appreciate every single person in my life who has tried to brighten my days.
  It's the little things that matter the most.
  —tinybuddha.com—

This little passage is truly my acknowledgements to my dearest friends who have never stopped encouraging me and are always there for me when I need them. Thank you so much for believing in me. This is my first - tiny book - but will be the first of many.

Also to my girls - who will be surprised to find out that their mom is now a published author. Surprise!!!

Unlocking The Magic of Crystals For Beginners

By: Sandy Soyke

"A Smile is a Curve that Sets Everything Straight"
– Phyllis Diller –

Introduction: How my Journey into Crystals Began

Hi - I'm Sandy and I am known for my smile by my family, friends and colleagues but they also know me as the Crystal Girl. My quest with exploring crystals started way back in 1988 when I started my work career at Howard County General Hospital where I met two amazing women who became my mentors and my lifelong friends: Marianne Crouse and Cindi Miller. Both of these women introduced me to crystals, their meanings, their powers of physical healing and protection along with how you will grow spiritually and psychically all with the magic of crystals. We would go to Crystal shows as often as they were available. Hunt out Crystal stores, attend workshops, lectures, you name it and we found every opportunity to learn about crystals. I was like a sponge soaking up as much as I could and loving every minute of it. I have always had an eye for crystals, gemstones sort of like a calling but I never knew why until I started learning more about them and how my life could be so different with crystals.

It's fascinating actually if you think about it; you are walking along a country side road, or hiking a trail in the mountains or even walking on a beach and you look down - there it is. You reach down to pick it up having no idea what you just found but only knowing that it is beautiful and you have never seen anything like it before. That's how it starts - your desire to learn - your desire to seek and find. You just picked up your first crystal and now you have discovered what this big beautiful magical earth has to offer. How can anything so beautiful come out of the earth? How is it made? Magic? Questions I still ask myself every single time I open the door to my Crystal Room. Yes - I have a Crystal Room. It is a room I go to when I need a break or just need to recharge and yes most definitely meditate. My Crystal room brings a feeling of peace over anyone who walks in there whether they actually believe in the magic of crystals or not. This my friends is what I want to unlock for you in my book. What I want to share with you. What I want you to get excited about just like I do when I find that perfect crystal and wonder how? How did that crystal come to be? How did it make it out of the ground like that? How is it so beautiful, so exquisite, so unique? This is the magic - the magic of crystals.

"The noblest art is that of making others happy."

~ P.T. Barnum ~

1

Crystals - A Little History, A Lot of Magic

Crystals have been a part of life here on earth for as long as people have been here on earth. Let me explain. People have always been drawn to beautiful stones sometimes not even knowing what they are; however, when they find one that catches their eye, it's a keeper. Why - because something about the stone makes you feel good. That's right and you can't explain it because it is just a feeling but you know that you have to keep it. That my friends is the crystal speaking to you. Don't laugh - it's true. If you find a crystal that you have that strong a connection to and you don't want to let it go, then yes it is speaking to you and yes it belongs to you. I call it magic because not only did you pick the crystal but the crystal also picked you. Magic!

For those of you who don't believe in magic, let me tell you about a magical incident that just happened to me regarding a crystal. I have friends in Canada where I choose my crystals and this particular day that is exactly what I was hoping to do. I was on their website looking at their newest crystals and I just happened to be on a page with a few pieces of fluorite towers on it. I picked one in particular to look at and brought it up on my screen. It was reduced because it had a tiny, tiny chip on the tip of the tower. You could have used a microscope to see it, that's how tiny it was. So I clicked back off the crystal and tried to look at the other fluorite towers. My screen went white and said "sorry this website is having trouble". I'm thinking to myself - well that's crazy I have been on this website for over 45 minutes now. So I clicked back onto the fluorite tower I was just looking at and it came back up. Once again, I tried to click onto the next picture - white screen again "sorry this website is having trouble". What is going on!! I went back into the picture of the fluorite again with the chip. This time I placed it in my cart and guess what happened? Yep you got it - the website was working fine and I went on to view the rest of the crystals. That piece of fluorite was not letting me leave before I put it in my cart. It wanted me to buy it. It had chosen me. Now when a crystal goes to those lengths to make you purchase it - you best do what it wants because it belongs to you. Magic - no doubt about it.

Crystals can be found everywhere whether it be in a cave, on the side of a mountain, by a bank of water, or in your backyard if you are living in a new development. Crystals come from the earth and are made from the earth's movements over hundreds and even thousands of years ago. Movements with the sun, wind, water all play a part with how crystals are formed, their colors and where we find them. It is truly a miracle of nature and one we should always treasure. Before crystals were discovered by man, some of these crystals were probably hidden in our Earth for over a million years just waiting to be discovered. Can you imagine some crystals can be as old as our Earth? Unbelievable right? Crystals - their history goes back far beyond our time. Yes - that is crazy but real and very fascinating.

Just to give you an example of how far back in time we are talking, let's go back about six thousand years ago, to the ancient Babylonians.

The Babylonians' believed crystals were given to them by the Planetary Gods whom they worshiped. The Babylonian people were magicians, while some were astrologers, but all were very strong believers in the power of crystals. So, they used crystals in their everyday life to help them predict the future, make magic potions and spells. Their crystals were used in any way that could improve or enhance their daily living because they believed each crystal held some sort of cosmic energy.

In history, it tells how emeralds, my beautiful birthstone, were once "sold in the markets of Babylon as early as 4,000 BCE. I get that though, how could anyone not be attracted to emeralds? Even the "Ancient Egyptians, (I will be talking about further), believed that emeralds were a gift from Thoth, the God of Wisdom. Rediscovered a hundred years ago in Egypt are ancient emerald mines thought to be some of the oldest in the world. They are known as Cleopatra's Mines, after the ancient queen's love of the stone.Emeralds were also talismans of Aristotle, Alexander the Great, Charlemagne, and the moguls of India."

Another crystal that is green but usually a lighter green is Aventurine. This stone has a history with the Tibetan monks and was used for the eyes in their statues. The monks believed it would "reveal the god's visionary powers" if they placed the crystals in the statues. It was also believed the crystal would "improve sight and enhance spiritual power."

Jade is yet another green stone. It is considered a noble stone throughout Asia. Jade is acknowledged for its connection with the sun and its "powerful yang energy." In Ancient China it does have a reputation as being a solution for all diseases. It is also said to bring whoever is wearing it riches and peace of mind. If you see a jade butterfly, and you know a couple that is getting married, it holds a special meaning for engaged couples. Let me explain: Here's how the legend is told -

"a young man, in pursuit of a butterfly, ventured into a private garden of a rich lord. Instead of being punished for his trespass, he ended up marrying the lord's daughter. A symbol of happily-ever-after-romance, bridegrooms often give their fiance's a jade butterfly to ensure a good marriage."

Peridot - the birthstone for August is also a green stone. It was "used in ancient civilization as a charm to ward off sorcery, evil spirits, and madness. Throughout the European medieval period, peridot was ground down into powder and sold in apothecary stores as an antidote for madness and nightmares."

Did you know that the "ancient scribes of the Old Testament noted that Noah's Ark was thought to be illuminated by one precious garnet, while later medieval crusaders wore garnets as amulets to protect them against attack." Pretty cool!

Of course, when talking about history and crystals we certainly can't forget Ancient Egypt. The Egyptians used crystals for just about everything from cosmetic purposes to improving their health. Lapis lazuli was one of the most popular crystals due to its gorgeous blue color, symbolizing the heavens. Ancient civilizations believed the crystal to contain the power of the gods. It was used by many to make jewelry and an "ultramarine dye" for the robes of priests and royalty. Many of the kings and queens of Egypt would actually use lapis lazuli to inlay their tombs since it is known for its protection powers. It was used to decorate the funeral mask of Pharaoh Tutankhamun.

Jasper was another favorite crystal of the Egyptians because it represented fire, life and blood. The crystal that represented fertility and new growth to the Egyptians was malachite. Also, the Egyptian pharaohs believed that malachite would make them wiser leaders, so they would line their headdresses with malachite. It was also ground into a powder and used as eye shadow because the Egyptians believed it would increase their sight and improve their spiritual insight. It is also believed that the Egyptians even placed crystals in their pyramid caps to "channel cosmic forces down through the geometric structures." Carnelian was used to reveal the Egyptian rank, "master builders wore carnelian, thought to be the stone of form and design."

Another crystal that was very popular with the Ancient Egyptians was rose quartz. The Egyptians would find rose quartz crystals and actually chisel those crystals, so they look like face masks and then use them on their faces. They did this because they believed rose quartz would help their appearance and keep them from looking old.

Rose Quartz beads were found that dated back as far as 7000 BCE, from the culture known as Mesopotamia, which is now the country we call Iraq.

Oh, and let's not forget the Ancient Greeks who also had their beliefs when it came to crystals. "Greeks believed that every piece of clear quartz crystal was water frozen by the Gods, and called it **crystallos**, meaning "**icicle**." Believe it or not, the Roman women would carry these crystals around in their hands on those hot dreadful days of summer to keep their hands nice and cool. Amazing don't you think?

"Clear Quartz was the key to the development of many ancient civilizations. A staple spiritual and magical tool for the Celts, Mayans, Aztecs, Egyptians and Native Americans, many believed these crystals to be alive, incarnations of the Divine. They were believed to have a great power for healing and for raising consciousness."

In Greek Mythology opals were used to attract fortune and good trade because they were associated with Hermes, the God of trade and travel. Wearing an agate ring to the Greeks would mean that you would be "favored by the Gods, while according to the Roman historian and writer, Pliny, the Persian magi burnished agate stones to avert storms. The magicians proved the crystal's power by throwing agate into a cauldron of boiling water, which would miraculously cool down."

Rose Quartz once again shows up in ancient history. According to one legend, when Adonis, lover of the Greek goddess Aphrodite, was attacked by the jealous Ares, God of war. Aphrodite tried to save Adonis and caught her arm on a thorn bush. As their mingled blood fell to earth, it stained clear quartz, the rose-pink color.

The opal which holds the colors of the rainbow in it also has a legend attached to it. "Ancient Aboriginal Australians believed that when the Creator came down to Earth on a rainbow, at the very spot where his foot touched the ground the stones came alive. Sparkling with all the colors of the rainbow, they became the stones we know as opals. Another Aboriginal legend tells of a gigantic opal-like Creator, who ruled the stars, love and gold mines."

Pyrite, most people call it "fool's gold" because of its color and sparkle. It is considered the stone of power and great magic. It has been used frequently by indigenous North American shamans. They carved pyrite into amulets and used natural stones for divination or for healing ceremonies and magical spells. Both the Incas of Peru and the Mexican Aztecs would polish large slabs or impressive pieces of pyrite into mirrors and use them for fortune telling and scrying. While one side was usually polished smooth, the opposite side was curved outward and often were engraved with distinctive symbolic scoring to summon spirits and oracular communications.

Smoky Quartz was "originally called morion when it was discovered and used by the Druids and Celts around 300 BCE". Believe it or not Smoky Quartz has become Scotland's "national gemstone". The Scottish Highlanders during their ceremonies actually used this stone as part of the crystals they placed in the handles of their ceremonial Scottish dagger, and yes, it is still used today as part of their uniform.

Tiger's Eye was used as an ancient talisman and was said to bring good luck and lots of great fortune to whoever wore it. The Ancient Egyptians also believed that Tiger's Eye communicated the power of the sun God Ra. Then we have the Romans who would carry Tiger's Eye into battle with them because they believed it would make them braver. What do you think? Did it work? It was thought to have "the power of not just the sun but the earth as well, and therefore, tiger's eye could help transform pure energy into practical reality and tangible success."

UNLOCKING THE MAGIC OF CRYSTALS FOR BEGINNERS

2

Crystals and Their Specific Healing Powers

In this chapter I am going to be going over the specific healing powers associated with the ten crystals that were given to you in Chapter Two. Now remember - just a word of advice - **Crystals are never intended to be a substitute for medical advice. If you are sick, please seek out the advice of your medical professional.**

Let's get started on helping you understand your ten crystals and how special their healing powers are to you.

Amethyst - This crystal has many healing powers which is probably why I have it in every room of my house. It is a very calming stone. It takes away negativity and brings a feeling of contentment. This is also the crystal you use when we need to stop something that is no longer good in our lives. Such as drinking, or working too much, or shopping too much, or smoking, anything at all that we need to stop. This crystal is used for treating what we call addictions no matter what kind or how simple they may be. This crystal carries with it a high frequency that can expel the negativity and it will put a protective shield of light around your body instead. Calm - you will feel very calm. Its calming focus on your body and mind brings about peace, love, courage and spiritual happiness. Amethyst can also wake up your imagination and your intuitive powers so that you can begin to come up with new ideas, plans, trips, wherever your imagination wants to take you. This is by far my favorite crystal.

Rose Quartz

Rose Quartz - This crystal is called the love crystal because it brings about love whenever it is needed. Whether it is self-love that you are searching for or unconditional love from a partner that you can't quite put your finger on yet, or just love for friends. This crystal will help you manifest the love, warmth and desire you need to find. This light pink crystal will bring peace, calm and love to a relationship. It will melt away all your fears, any anxiety you may have thus leaving you feeling very relaxed, carefree and open to love. It will raise your self-esteem, restore confidence, release stress, tension, and anger; and help keep that green eyed monster in check. Rose Quartz with its calming and reassuring abilities is also a great crystal to have in times of grief. Rose Quartz can resolve negativity and protect against environmental pollution, replacing it with loving vibes.

CRYSTALS AND THEIR SPECIFIC HEALING POWERS

Labradorite - This crystal was discovered in 1770 in Labrador, Canada which is how it got its name. Labradorite is of course known as the "stone of magic" because it is used by magicians. It is also used by anyone else who wants complete change, self-discovery and divine adventure. It is known for its supernatural powers, its power of protection, its fearlessness, and for those who want to travel between worlds, you can do that safely with this crystal. Labradorite will awaken your psychic abilities, open up your deepest imagination, and definitely bring out your adventurous side. This crystal is the crystal to have in your collection for healers all around this big world of ours.

CRYSTALS AND THEIR SPECIFIC HEALING POWERS

Lapis Lazuli - This crystal is used for communication. It is a great stone for promoting confidence and grace and will definitely ease communication breakdowns or issues you may have with family, friends, giving speeches or any kind of communication. It will increase your prophetic dreams giving you meaning to them, increase clairvoyance to understand and guide. Lapis Lazuli has the power to seek out honesty and compassion in your communication so you can let go of any anger you are holding on to from your past. Which sometimes is hard for us to do. This crystal will help us release that anger and talk freely and solve our conflict. Great crystal for protection also. If you choose to meditate with this crystal, it will help you relieve stress and give you peace and serenity. One of my favorites too because it will help ease headaches, anxiety and will help relax your nervous system. Just hold your lapis on the area that you are having trouble with, in my case it is always my head, and just relax while the crystal does the rest. It also tends to work for earaches and if my eyes are worn out from reading or watching television. Once the crystal stops being cool, usually I start feeling better. Try it and let me know how it works for you.

Malachite - This crystal has amazing protection powers. This crystal can transfer negative energies into positive energies. It also works as a sort of a magnetic force sucking up harmful toxins from the air.

Malachite will also clean the air of unhealthy radiation from your televisions, computers, or microwaves. Just place a couple of pieces in whatever room you have these appliances in, and it will protect you from these dangerous rays. Also, if you love to fly or just take the occasional trip for work or vacation, don't forget to take a piece of malachite with you on the plane. Remember malachite will take care of any radiation you might encounter on the plane and help with travel sickness and fear of flying. Malachite will also work on your body if you have worked out at the gym, in your garden or just finished running a 5k and noticed your foot seems a bit swollen. Use malachite by just placing a piece on top of a cloth of some sort and put it on your foot. It will help with the inflammation. Good news for women - it will also help you with menstrual cramps each month by just placing a piece of malachite right on your stomach while lying down and relaxing. It could also help with toothaches by just placing a piece on your face where the tooth hurts. This crystal has the energy to uplift your immune system, improve your circulation, trigger regeneration of cell growth, help your liver work the best it can and will also help your blood pressure stay in check. Now remember though, as I said before, **please consult your doctor for any medical problems you may have. Even though this crystal and many others can help you, I would never recommend to you that they replace seeing a doctor for your healthcare needs.** Just one last important note about malachite - it manifests its very deep healing green color of "nature and represents the beauty of flowers, trees, roots and plants."

Smoky Quartz - This crystal is a great crystal for grounding. It also works for getting rid of negativity. Let's say you are driving down the road and someone cuts you off. What's the first thing you want to do? Yep - I am with you - yell, right? Well keep a piece of smoky quartz in your car and that will help you control your road rage and keep the negativity at bay. Plus, since it is a stone of protection, it will help keep you from having an accident when you do get cut off. Smoky quartz helps you get rid of stress and will also help if you are having trouble falling asleep at night. Just put one in your bedroom so you can go to sleep easier. You can also use smoky quartz in any room in your house where you have conversations, and the mood suddenly changes, or people might start getting a little hostile or angry. The smoky quartz can lift all that negativity and start bringing positive thoughts and energy back into the room. Smoky quartz also works for bullying in the workplace. Just place a piece on your desk and it will help you to remain calm, stay focused and complete your day's work.

Yellow Tiger's Eye - This crystal is a crystal of luck and bravery especially when beginning new adventures. It sparks your creative juices, your will power to begin again and to stick with these scary but awesome new changes in your life. Tiger's eye can help you with a change in your lifestyle. Say you need to change your eating habits or start exercising or just stop working so many hours, this crystal can boost your willpower and energy levels so that you can stick with those changes and make them work for you. Place a piece of tiger's eye in a major room in your house where you have important family meetings, and this will help keep everyone calm and encourage peace and less arguing. It will help your family stay more in tuned with each other. A happy family is the best gift of all.

Pyrite - This crystal, believe it or not is known as a "masculine stone" because it is a stone of "action and ambition, perfect for attracting wealth and abundance." I'm not sure why that equates to a man but so be it. I think it is more about its shapes and color than anything else. Pyrite is also seen in cubes and is always shiny and gold. Who knows - right? Anyway, the crystal itself will help you overcome anxiety or any destructive tendencies you may have. It will help you begin to form a new beginning for yourself where you will forge ahead and take charge of what you want in your career and your life.Keeping a piece on your desk at work will help relieve your stress, mental confusion and just plain tiredness and give you increased energy and boost your enthusiasm.

Just a word to the wise - this is one crystal I have in my collection because of its unique powers but I cannot touch it. It is the only crystal in my collection that I can say that about. Maybe because the energy that comes from pyrite is electric. I can't quite put my finger on it; but when I hold it, I immediately get dizzy and feel like I am going to pass out. This crystal packs a punch with its power. You will have to let me know if any of you have any changes once you start working with it. I would be very curious to hear about your results.

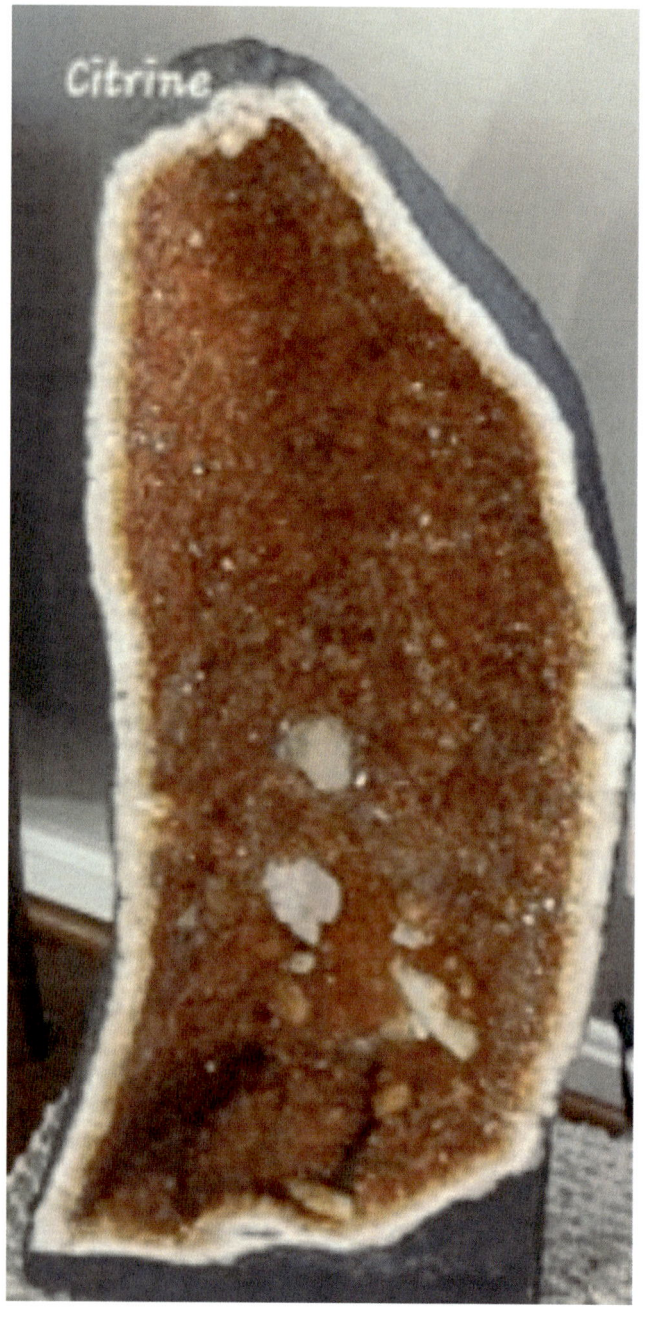

Citrine - This crystal is known as the "success stone" mainly because it is known to bring good luck in everything you choose to do.It is also referred to as the stone of abundance and manifestation, because it attracts wealth and prosperity along with success and anything else that may be fabulous. This crystal also encourages being generous to others and sharing in your success and good fortune. This crystal can encourage you to spend wisely by strengthening your intuition. It also will let you get rid of past anger, the fears of lack of and all those destructive thoughts floating around in your head that are blocking abundance from entering in and helping you to enjoy your new way of thinking. If you can bring this new light into your life, you will enjoy an abundance of opportunities and create the kind of life you have always wanted for yourself and your family. If you can activate your imagination, then that is the first step toward your quest to manifestation. **You need to first imagine it before you can bring it into reality. So, hold your citrine in your hand and envision whatever it is you want to change. Envision the change going in the citrine and the charge of the crystal with the energy its producing is so powerful that now you can actually see your ideas spring into action, and you can watch everything take place.** You now have the energy and creativity to set your change into motion. **Go for it. Communicate and Create - you can do it!**

Clear Quartz - This crystal is transparent and clear to sometimes a milky white color. The crystals that are clear usually are full of rainbows which when you hold it up to the light shine throughout the entire crystal. This crystal can also be called the Rock Crystal. You guessed it, because it looks like a rock. Clear Quartz is used for healing and also for anyone looking to grow spiritually. It is probably the most popular crystal and the most easily recognizable anywhere you go on earth. It is known for its ability to magnify the power that other crystals hold, making their power even greater. So, if you are wearing another crystal, why not wear clear quartz with it to get that extra punch of power. Clear Quartz can improve your mental clarity so it can let you see things clearer and keep your emotions in check. This is my second favorite crystal. I use this crystal for everything from headaches to backaches.

I use it when I am dizzy and need to balance myself, so I don't fall, which seems to happen a lot lately since I had Covid back in December 2020.

CRYSTALS AND THEIR SPECIFIC HEALING POWERS

Clear quartz restores balance to the body, strengthens your metabolism, and is a powerful anti-inflammatory.

"The Environment is where we all meet; where all have a mutual interest; it is the one thing all of us share."

–Lady Bird Johnson–

3

How to Recharge Your Crystals

Let's get started on how to cleanse your crystals because there are several different ways to do this. I will give you some of my favorites and then you can choose which ones best suit your lifestyle and your time frame.

Moonlight Bath: This was my first crystal cleanse and my personal favorite. Of course, when I was using this method, I only had a few crystals in my collection. Now I couldn't use this method because it would take me a month to move all my crystals outside. So, let's talk about how you cleanse your crystals. The moon's energy helps cleanse and charge your crystals. The moon's light is the brightest and most energetically strongest during the full moon. Just place your crystals on a ceramic or glass plate, on your deck table, on your deck steps, in your backyard. Wherever they will get the moon's powerful rays and then let the moon do its job.

Water Bath: With this cleanse just place your crystals in a clean glass bowl or container and fill the container with either spring water, mineral water or purified water. I don't recommend using just plain tap water. Let the crystals soak overnight in the water. Or you can use a bowl of fresh rainwater if you happen to have saved some from the last rainfall. If you live by a lake or a stream, feel free to hold your crystals under the water for about five to ten minutes and visualize the negativity washing away with the flow of the water. Just be sure not to let the crystals wash away with the water. One important item I would like to say about Malachite. Malachite consumes so much as a crystal because of its healing powers so you should probably cleanse this crystal on a regular basis if you use it regularly. Cleaning it continuously with water will unfortunately cause the crystal to fall into pieces. Now if this does happen, you can take the crystal out to your yard and bury it because your crystal has finished its job and is ready to be returned to the earth.

Salt Bath: Washing your crystals in salt works well because salt not only absorbs unwanted energies, but it will purify them also. If you live by the beach, salt water is plentiful. If you don't, just make salt water at home by using a clean glass container and salt. I use pink Himalayan salt. I use about 1 to 2 tablespoons of salt for about every 8 ounces of water. Let your crystals soak for at least 24 hours. After you take your crystals out of the salt water, don't forget to rinse them with fresh water to remove any salt residue.

Rice Bath: Ok this one is easy, just don't use the rice afterwards. Get a container big enough to hold your crystals. See if you can find a big glass serving bowl and then put the crystals in. Cover them completely with brown rice and let them sit overnight. The rice works its magic by absorbing the bad vibes from your crystals. By morning your crystals will be cleansed. Now don't forget to throw the rice out because you certainly don't want to eat any bad mojo.

Burying Your Crystals: You can bury your crystals in your backyard or if you live in an apartment, bury them in your favorite flowerpot. When you bury your crystals in the ground, you are returning them to the earth; so, it is the vibration of the earth that will be recharging your crystals. I usually leave them buried for at least 48 hours. Sometimes depending on the crystals and the last time I cleansed, I might just leave them in the ground for the entire cycle of the moon, which is about a month. Just remember where your crystals are in your yard so you can remember to dig them up when the time is right.

Singing Bowl: I have been collecting crystals since 1988 so my Crystal Room is full of crystals of all shapes and sizes. Needless to say, I am not going to be able to use most of these methods unless I do a little here and a little there. So, I bought a singing bowl. I know - you are thinking - a singing bowl - what is a singing bowl? A singing bowl is a metal bowl that by using a soft mallet and going around and around the bowl can send a high pitch cleansing sound to your crystals to cleanse them. I use the bowl for only about 2 to 5 minutes which is quite enough vibration time to cleanse your crystals. Do not put your crystals inside the singing bowl while you are using it because it might crack your crystals. This is my favorite way of cleansing my crystals. Give it a try. It's not only fun but the bowl sounds nice.

So there are other methods of cleansing crystals but these are the easiest one's for you to use when your collection is limited to around ten crystals.

Also, before I leave the subject of cleansing, I wanted to let you know that three of the crystals in your crystal collection are **self-cleansing crystals**: the **Amethyst**, the **Citrine** and the **Smoky Quartz**. Now just because they are self-cleansing doesn't mean you still can't cleanse them. I do this because I think all crystals can use a cleansing once in a while and it's a great way to just take care of them.

There are other crystals that are self-cleansing but since they are not part of the ten crystals I gave you in this book, I will give you those in my next adventure. My next book will get into additional ways to cleanse crystals, using crystals when meditating, learning about chakras and crystals, and more cleansing ways. There is so much to learn about how you can enhance your life with crystals, and I am looking forward to sharing it with you in my next book.

4

Understanding What Crystals Are Right for You

I know what you are thinking - oh my gosh where do I begin? How do I start building my crystal collection? I don't know what crystals I need. Well don't panic because I am here to help you and we will conquer this together. I am going to give you the top ten essential crystals that are a must in everyone's collection. I will also give you the reason I have selected them for you. Let's get started.

Amethyst - color = deep purple

This crystal is important to have in your collection because it helps rid your life of negative influences. Negative energy. When you go into a crystal store, you will see an Amethyst geode probably standing in the corner of the room. The reason for that is because the Amethyst is there to rid the room of any negative energy that may walk into the store. My house has more amethyst in it than any other crystal I own. Amethyst is by far my favorite crystal.

Amethyst comes "from Argentina, Bolivia, Brazil, Canada, Russia, Siberia, South Korea, Sri Lanka, United States, Uruguay, and Zambia"

Rose Quartz - color = light pink
    This crystal belongs in everyone's collection. It is known as the love stone. It improves all types of love, including the way you love yourself, others and that special someone. It will work its magic on your self-esteem as it promotes positive energy and restores your confidence.

Rose Quartz comes from "Brazil, Germany, India, Madagascar, United States"

Labradorite - color = iridescent blue green …. reminds me of Peacock Feathers
    This crystal is as magical as the colors itself. When and if you want to explore your magical side, this is the crystal to use. It is called the "Stone of Magic". "According to an ancient legend, the Inuit people believed Labradorite was formed by the northern lights, or aurora borealis, that shone down on the shores of Labrador in Canada. "Labradorescence" was captured inside the rocks on the shore, resulting in the fiery reflection that appears on this stone's surface."

Labradorite comes "from Afghanistan, Canada, Chile, India, Italy, Madagascar, Mongolia, Pakistan, Russia, United States, Uruguay

Lapis Lazuli - color = deep, deep, royal blue
    Lapis is needed in your collection because it is the stone of communication. It helps you to be able to talk freely and say what it is you want to say without stumbling over your words. Good communication is needed in all we do. Also, just a reminder, this crystal was used for its power way back in Ancient Egypt.

Lapis Lazuli comes "from Afghanistan, Canada, Chile, India, Italy,

Madagascar, Mongolia, Pakistan, Russia, United States and Uruguay.

Malachite - color = dark green
  Malachite is a must have for your collection. Don't forget this was a crystal also used by Ancient Egyptians like Cleopatra in her eyeliner. Malachite is a stone of protection and good health.

Malachite come "from Australia, Chile, Germany, Mexico, South Africa, Romania, Russia, United States, Zaire

Smoky Quartz - color = translucent brownish gray - almost black
  Smoky Quartz is another crystal that works its magic of protection on us. Having it in your home helps protect your home from theft, from any kind of damage, or accidents. This stone works as a negativity blocker. The perfect stone for anyone to hang on to and have one at work and in their house.

Smoky Quartz comes "from Australia, Brazil, Madagascar, Mozambique, Scotland, Switzerland, United States

Yellow Tiger's Eye - color = usually streaked with brown and yellow colors
  This crystal has many uses with the most common being protection against evil intentions from others. However, it is also known as the good luck stone because it gives you the ability to discriminate between what you really need to have and what you really want to have thus making sure you make wise choices and not bad choices. It is said to bring the wearer a steady flow of abundance. It might give you the extra boost you might need in a meeting, on a date, making a hard decision.

Can be worn or carried daily.

Yellow Tiger's Eye comes "from Australia, Brazil, China, India, Myanmar, South Africa, Spain, United States

Iron Pyrite - color = shiny gold sometimes has quartz crystals included

Pyrite is often referred to as "fool's gold" because of its color and the fact that it resembles gold to the everyday person. The crystal got its name from the Greek word **pyr** meaning "fire". Iron pyrite was named for its ability to emit sparks when pieces were struck against each other. It is known in different parts of the world as the 'stone of health" due to its positive healing powers.

Iron Pyrite comes "from Australia, France, Germany, Italy, Peru, Russia, Taiwan, United States

Citrine - color = a golden yellow like the sun

Citrine is often created by heating amethyst and believe it or not it tends to enhance the crystal's power rather than diluting it. This crystal is often called the "success stone" because it is said to bring the owner good luck in everything they try to accomplish. Also, this crystal is special in that it never needs to be cleansed as it dispels all negative energy and can clear unwanted energies such as geopathic stress and psychic pollution from the environment. "Natural Citrine" is a lighter yellow and purer in color and is definitely the ultimate manifestation stone, because it will empower your imagination, and remove all negativity.

Citrine comes "mainly from Brazil, but can also be found in Argentina, France, Spain, and Scotland

I saved the best crystal for last. The one that everyone needs - no doubt whatsoever.

Are you ready?

It's **Clear Quartz!**

Clear Quartz - color = clear - colorless but sometimes full of rainbows

Clear Quartz is the one crystal you need in your crystal box above all others. It is the one crystal that plays well with others. Let's say if you were in a band and all the instruments were there and you were just waiting for the speakers to be set up. That is what your Clear Quartz is - it would be your speakers to all your other crystals. You can use your clear quartz with any other crystal to help magnify what your other crystal does. That's how great clear quartz is, and you need to keep it around you at all times. It is used to connect you with your higher self and your intuition. It is known as the "Master Healer" and the "High Channeler" and it does work just as hard or harder for you with your other crystals to get the results you need.

Clear Quartz comes "from Brazil, Canada, China, Germany, Madagascar, Peru, South Africa, United States.

Before I leave this chapter on **Understanding What Crystals are Right for You**, I just want you to know that there are hundreds, thousands of different crystals out there to explore and get to know. My crystal room is probably full of thousands of crystals. However, if I tried to write about even 50 of them, I would never finish writing because there is so much to write about each crystal. Eventually, you must pick a stopping point. So, I picked the crystals that I started my collection with when I started so many years ago. I promise I will write another book with more crystals, unique crystals like you have never seen before and I will keep your journey with crystals moving forward just like mine continues to move forward. Crystals are fascinating and each day I learn more and more about them. I guess what amazes me the most on my journey is seeing how these crystals actually are formed from inside this great big, beautiful world we live in and how many crystals are still out there yet to be discovered. That is the best part of my journey and why it can never end.

Petrified Wood

"We do not inherit the Earth from our Ancestors; We borrow it from our Children"

–American Proverb–

5

Quick Easy Crystal Guide for Common Health Issues

In this chapter, I will be discussing common health issues that we all suffer from once in a while and what crystals can help us in those situations.

Headaches - Clear Quartz or Amethyst - lay in a dark room with the crystal on your forehead and imagine the crystal melting away your pain. When the crystal starts feeling warm, your headache should have moved away from your head. I use my Clear Quartz all the time for my headaches especially while I am driving because it works even when I am not laying down.

Backaches - Citrine or Smoky Quartz - lay down and ask someone to gently rub your back with either of these crystals until your still feeling better. You can also wear these crystals too.

Fatigue - Citrine - wear it continuously maybe as a necklace and make sure it is touching your skin.

Indigestion - Citrine - helps you feel better if you have problems with your stomach and/or your intestines. You can wear Citrine or you can lay down and place it on your stomach.

Addictions - Amethyst - definitely your go to crystal for addictions not matter what kind. If you need to stop something that you have been having trouble stopping, pull out the Amethyst. It will help.

Menstrual Cramps - Malachite - you can wear it or lay down and place it where your pain is either your back or lower abdomen.

Ulcers, Diabetes, Gallstones, Constipation - Tiger's Eye or Citrine - you can wear it or place it on whatever area is bothering you, and leave it on that area for at least 20 minutes while trying to relax.

High Blood Pressure, Bronchitis, Asthma - Rose Quartz - you can wear it continuously or place it on the area that needs help and just relax for at least 30 minutes.

Sore Throat, Cold, Sore Neck - Lapis Lazuli - you can wear this crystal around your neck as a necklace against your skin or place it on the area where you need the help the most while laying down and relaxing.

Chronic Exhaustion - Labradorite or Clear Quartz - you can wear these crystals around your neck, or on your finger as a ring, or you can carry them with you.

Problems with knees, hips, ankles or feet - Smoky Quartz - you can wear this crystal or carry it or you can place it on the area where you need the crystal to help you the most.

Insomnia, nightmares - Amethyst - place an amethyst on your nightstand before you go to bed at night. You can even place a small amethyst underneath your pillow to help you sleep.

Now, this is only a small sampling of the healing powers that crystals can help you with. I kept it to only the ten crystals that I have started your crystal collection to make it a little easier. Again, let me stress to you - **If you have any medical issues, please consult your medical doctor. Crystals are not here to take the place of your medical doctor.** Most people, myself included, use crystals to help balance ourselves, improve our well-being, and bring serenity and tranquility to our lives. Now can't we all use a bit more of all these things in our lives?

Credits

Photographs of crystals in my book were taken by my daughter, Jeni Barnette with help from Eden Crushong, my granddaughter. Also, Jeni was kind enough to help place the pictures into my book when I couldn't get them to cooperate with me. Everyone knows I am not the best with technology.

I would also love to give a great big Thank You to my granddaughter, Addison who gave up some precious time on our weekend away to help me copy and paste my book all over again into a very stubborn program. We were able to just about complete the book with her computer skills and she was having so much fun helping me.

Also, I am sure before this book gets published my son-in-law, Dave Wilhelm will share a part in getting this published, due to my lack of computer knowledge, so I want to give a shout out to him also.

A lot of my unusual crystals were purchased through my friends, Sabrina and Ross at Earth Family Crystals - www.earthfamilycrystals.com. Check them out - you will be pleasantly surprised. They have one-of-a-kind pieces that you won't find anywhere else.

Also, check out The Bridge Healing Center - I have also been buying crystals and jewelry from the founder and my dear friend, whom I have known since before she graduated and became famous - Anne Marie

Rose. She has done a terrific job with her stores and her business. Check out her location at 400 N. Center Street in Westminster, Maryland.

Selected Bibliography

Anderson, Emily, The Essential Book of Crystals, 2021 by Sirius Publishing

McCann, Colleen, CRYSTAL RX, 2018 by HarperCollins books

Earth Family Crystals, Sabrina & Ross - earthfamilycrystals.com

Rodenbeck, Christina, Crystals, 2014 by Bounty Books

About the Author

Sandy currently resides in Hanover, PA with her dog Chloe and her African Gray, Scarlett. Sandy recently retired from the healthcare field after 32 years. She began her passion of crystals back in 1987 and has been learning and collecting ever since. She enjoys sharing her crystals with her family and friends. Sandy also enjoys writing and collecting LP's. Sandy also enjoys spending time with her 4 daughters and her grandchildren.

Made in the USA
Las Vegas, NV
23 September 2023